TV COOKS

Keith Floyd

COOKS

Barbecues

Photographs by Philip Webb

BBC BOOKS

Published by BBC Books,
an imprint of BBC Consumer Publishing.
BBC Worldwide Limited, Woodlands,
80 Wood Lane, London W12 0TT.

The recipes in this book first appeared in:
Floyd's American Pie
© Keith Floyd 1989
Floyd on Britain and Ireland
© Keith Floyd 1988
Floyd on Fire
© Keith Floyd 1986
Floyd on Fish
© Keith Floyd 1985
Floyd on France
© Keith Floyd 1987

We would like to thank the Absolute Press for allowing us to
adapt recipes from **Floyd on Fire** and **Floyd on Fish**.

This edition first published 1997
© Keith Floyd 1997
The moral right of the author
has been asserted

ISBN 0 563 38346 1

Edited by Pam Mallender
Designed by DW Design
Photographs by Philip Webb
Styling by Helen Payne
Home Economists Jane Stevenson and Fran Ward
Author photograph by Julian Nieman

Set in New Caledonia and Helvetica
Printed and bound in France by Imprimerie Pollina s.a.
Colour separations by Radstock Reproductions Limited,
Midsomer Norton
Cover printed in France by Imprimerie Pollina s.a.

Cover and frontispiece: Chicken Kebabs with Oregano.

CONTENTS

RECIPE NOTES

Eggs are size 2.
Wash all fresh produce before preparation and peel as necessary.
Spoon measurements are level. Always use proper measuring spoons:
1 teaspoon = 5ml and 1 tablespoon = 15ml.
Never mix metric and imperial measures in one recipe. Stick to one or the other.

HANDY CONVERSION TABLES

Weight		Volume		Linear	
15g	½oz	30ml	1fl oz	5mm	⅛in
25g	1oz	50ml	2fl oz	10mm/1cm	½in
40g	1½oz	100ml	3½fl oz	2cm	¾in
55g	2oz	125ml	4fl oz	2.5cm	1in
85g	3oz	150ml	5fl oz (¼ pint)	5cm	2in
115g	4oz	175ml	6fl oz	7.5cm	3in
140g	5oz	200ml	7fl oz (⅓ pint)	10cm	4in
175g	6oz	225ml	8fl oz	13cm	5in
200g	7oz	250ml	9fl oz	15cm	6in
225g	8oz	300ml	10fl oz (½ pint)	18cm	7in
250g	9oz	350ml	12fl oz	20cm	8in
280g	10oz	400ml	14fl oz	23cm	9in
350g	12oz	425ml	15fl oz (¾ pint)	25cm	10in
375g	13oz	450ml	16fl oz	28cm	11in
400g	14oz	500ml	18fl oz	30cm	12in
425g	15oz	600ml	20fl oz (1 pint)		
450g	1lb	700ml	1¼ pints		

Oven temperatures		
225F	110C	GAS ¼
250F	120C	GAS ½
275F	140C	GAS 1
300F	150C	GAS 2
325F	160C	GAS 3
350F	180C	GAS 4
375F	190C	GAS 5
400F	200C	GAS 6
425F	220C	GAS 7
450F	230C	GAS 8
475F	240C	GAS 9

Weight (continued):
550g	1¼lb
750g	1lb 10oz
900g	2lb
1kg	2¼lb
1.3kg	3lb
1.8kg	4lb
2.25kg	5lb

Volume (continued):
850ml	1½ pints
1 litre	1¾ pints
1.2 litres	2 pints
1.3 litres	2¼ pints
1.4 litres	2½ pints
1.7 litres	3 pints
2 litres	3½ pints
2.5 litres	4½ pints

Ⓥ   **Suitable for vegetarians**

⒡   **Low fat**

❊   **Suitable for freezing**

For millions a fitted kitchen is an absolute necessity. There is nothing wrong with that, but many people in the rest of the world do not have this luxury, or perhaps hindrance, because cooking is the simple matter of applying heat to raw food. The most exquisite meals can be created over some burning twigs by the side of a lake or grilled over charcoal in a makeshift barbecue made from an old car wheel.

When I was only a boy I grilled perch over beech twigs by the side of a Somerset lake. I have since had grilled beef ribs under the Southern Cross, stir-fried snake over charcoal in Vietnam, barbecued tiger fish on the banks of the Zambezi and grilled sardines under the setting sun in Spain.

Barbecuing, whether you use natural resources or one of the wide range of portable, built-in or disposable barbecues available today, gives you a culinary simplicity, pleasure and excitement that can't be matched in the kitchen.

You are outside, nature is around you, wood is burning, herbs perfume the air. Cooking outdoors is the absolute essence of total freedom. It is just you and mankind's first civilised experience: fire and food.

Keith Floyd

INGREDIENTS

Aubergines

These are also known as eggplants and are available most of the year. Look for those with bright, firm, shiny skin without any blemishes. The stalk should be green and fresh looking. Store in the fridge after buying.

Fennel

There are two types of fennel plant. The feathery leaves of one are used as a herb while the bulbous root of Florence fennel is eaten as a vegetable. The seeds of both are used as a spice. Herb or sweet fennel is a classical flavouring for fish – especially oily varieties where it counteracts the richness – and in marinades, soups and sauces. Dried sweet fennel root is also available. Florence fennel looks somewhat like a squashed celery stalk and most of its feathery fronds are chopped off before it is sold. Choose mature, well-rounded bulbs. Cut surfaces will brown when exposed to the air so drop into acidulated water if you are not using immediately.

Herbs and spices

Basil: fresh basil is a fabulous herb. It is excellent freshly chopped over cooked meat, or indeed crushed with garlic, salt and olive oil and poured over grilled chicken, lamb or fish – especially prawns, crayfish and scallops. Never use dried or powdered basil – OK, it smells of eau de Cologne, but do you really want your food to taste of aftershave? Just buy a plant and grow it on the window ledge.
Coriander: fresh coriander makes a splendid change from parsley, especially over lamb and pork kebabs. The seeds, quite different in taste from the leaves, are great with grilled fish and dishes of a spicy nature.
Cumin seeds: whether crushed, whole or ground, these are great especially with grilled fish such as tuna or mackerel or with meat such as lamb and beef. They have a distinctive mildly hot, sweetish flavour.
Ginger: fresh root ginger or ground ginger is magnificent in marinades for lamb, chicken and pork.
Mint: finely chopped, this is exquisite with lamb kebabs and koftas or in Moroccan dishes of beef.
Rosemary: the flavour of rosemary is very strong but it goes well with beef, pork, lamb, veal, chicken and some fish, particularly oily ones such as red mullet, anchovies and sardines. The best rosemary is to be found on the roadsides of Provence where the hot sun pumps it full of flavour.
Sage: with this in the garden, so the proverb says, one has no need of a doctor. This splendid herb,which is as good dried as it is fresh, is particularly good with fish, vegetables and pork.

Sweetcorn

This originated in America but is now grown all over the world. The cob's sweet, nutty flavour is at its best just after picking. Choose cobs with creamy, tightly packed kernels. If buying in the husk make sure that this is soft and tender and pale green with a bloom on it. The corn silk should be brown, fine and silky.

EQUIPMENT

Barbecues

There are many types of barbecue on the market today including all-in-one, take anywhere, disposable ones which you use once, then throw away.
Brazier: this is the basic type of barbecue, portable with detachable legs. The more sophisticated models have windshields or hoods and some come equipped with a rôtisserie.
Rôtisserie grill: this has the facility for spit-roasting as well as grilling. The rack height is adjustable as is the height of the spit itself. This is a barbecue for serious outdoor cooks.
Permanent garden grill: this is ideal for the barbecue fiend. There is something very special about cooking on a grill that is actually part of the outdoors. Make sure you position your construction at an angle to the

prevailing wind and set the grate carrying the fire above a metal tray. This can then catch the ash as it falls and also provide good ventilation. Line the interior of the grill with firebricks. DIY kits for permanent grills are now widely available, so take a look round.

Hibachi: very cheap to buy, this quite sturdy cast-iron portable grill sells in its thousands year in and year out. It comes in various sizes and specifications and is perfect for taking on holiday – along with a copy of this book, of course. Unlike the brazier type, the fire is laid on a grate rather than on the bottom of a fire bowl, thus allowing airflow under the fire which can be controlled by means of vents.

Kettle grill: this has a number of advantages over the more basic portable barbecues. The food is surrounded by heat and is cooked evenly and consequently at greater speed. Flare-ups caused by fat dripping on to the coals are far less likely, and food can be cooked even in the worst of weather conditions. Various types of kettle grills also incorporate a rôtisserie. The rack, however, is not always adjustable, so the heat can only be regulated by the use of vents.

Basting brushes

These are essential for basting food as it cooks to keep it moist. Choose long-handled ones if possible.

Cook's knives

If you are going to prepare your own fish you will need a fish filleting knife and a blunt knife for scaling. A large cook's knife will come in useful for chopping vegetables, and when preparing lobsters, and a smaller one will be handy for more fiddly jobs. A serrated fruit knife is also a good investment.

Drip tray

This is an invaluable aid to cooking outdoors, usually made of tin foil. It should be placed under the food to catch the juices, which can then be used either to baste the food or as the basis for a sauce with which to accompany the dish. Surround the drip tray with charcoal, varying the amount, depending on whether you require a fierce and intense heat or a longer and more gentle cooking process.

Fuel

There is a variety of fuel on the market. Shun all charcoal substitutes and use only the finest lumpwood charcoal or high-quality briquettes. If you are lucky enough to have fruit trees in your garden, then the dried cuttings from these will make a superb aromatic fuel. Remember, artificially flavoured fuels are to barbecuing as pot noodles are to haute cuisine.

Grips

Metal hinged grips are great for keeping fish whole when it is being turned and for cooking and turning several chops or steaks together.

Oven gloves

Not only do they prevent burns from spitting fat, you can get closer to the food if the fire is very hot.

Skewers

Use metal or wooden ones. Do soak wooden skewers in water before use, or they are likely to char and burn at the same time as the food.

Tongs

Keep a selection for manoeuvring food around the grill.

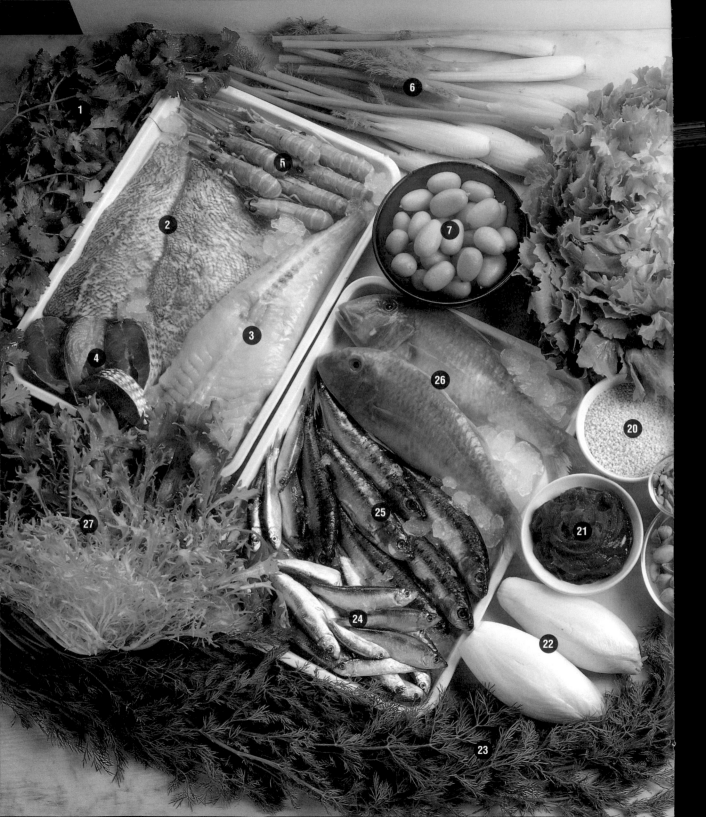

1. Fresh coriander
2. Bream fillets
3. Monkfish
4. Grey mullet steaks
5. Dublin Bay prawns
6. Fennel
7. Kumquats
8. Escarole
9. Lamb's lettuce
10. Pork fillet
11. Spare ribs
12. Fresh bay leaves
13. Mint
14. Salted anchovies
15. Goat's cheese
16. Cayenne pepper
17. Artichoke hearts
18. Pistachios
19. Cardamom
20. Sesame seeds
21. Red bean paste
22. Chicory
23. Fresh dill
24. Sprats
25. Sardines
26. Red mullet
27. Frisée

1. Oven gloves
2. Drip tray
3. Hinged circular grip for small fish
4. Ladle
5. Metal spatula
6. Tongs
7. Slotted spoon
8. Hinged grip for meat
9. Portable round barbecue
10. Hinged fish-shaped grip
11. Portable barbecue
12. Lumpwood charcoal
13. Wooden skewers
14. Metal skewers
15. Basting brush
16. Selection of cook's knives
17. Disposable barbecue

Starters

GRILLED GOAT'S CHEESE

For hungry people this superbly simple recipe might be used as a starter or a savoury in a lengthy meal. For others, grilled cheeses served with toasted genuine wholemeal bread and a crisp salad of chicory, endives and red lettuce, well dressed with a good olive oil and garlic and washed down with chilled rosé, will make a delightful lunchtime or evening snack.

Serves 4

4 individual goat's cheeses, not too hard and not too soft

4 tbsp olive oil

1 tsp coarse ground black pepper

1 tbsp fresh rosemary spikes

1 Cut a cross in both sides of each cheese and paint with the olive oil, then press both sides of the cheese into a mixture of the pepper and rosemary.
2 Barbecue lightly over the fire until the cheeses turn golden and start to ooze in the middle.

Nutrition notes per serving: *204 calories, Protein 7g, Carbohydrate 2g, Fat 19g, Saturated fat 2g, Fibre none, Added sugar none, Salt 0.60g*

TIP

If you are lucky enough to buy unpasteurised individual French goat's cheeses while on holiday, or from a really good cheese shop at home, so much the better. But if all else fails buy the little rolls or rounds now available in supermarkets. Much better still, when you can buy a couple of dozen genuine ones preserve them by popping them into an airtight jar with whole black peppercorns, a couple of dried chillies, a bay leaf or two and a few sprigs of fresh rosemary and thyme, then cover with olive oil. Eat raw or grilled at your will.

BARBECUED MARINATED PEPPERS ⓥ

This is a truly delicious summer starter served with fresh crunchy bread.

Serves 4

2 red and 2 green peppers

olive oil, to cover

freshly ground black pepper

sea salt

dash of white wine vinegar

1 You can either pop the peppers into a hot oven for 20 minutes until the skins start to blacken, or cook over the barbecue coals, turning from time to time. Remove from the heat and allow to cool slightly, then carefully peel off the skins. Cut off the bottoms and pull out the pith and pips.
2 When cool, cut into strips, and cover with olive oil, season and add the wine vinegar. Chill in the fridge for an hour or two before serving.

Nutrition notes per serving: *96 calories, Protein 1g, Carbohydrate 7g, Fat 7g, Saturated fat 1g, Fibre 2g, Added sugar none, Salt 0.51g*

Meat

FLOYD'S BARBECUED LAMB WITH MEYER LEMON SAUCE

I'm quite proud of this simple little dish, created entirely on the spur of the moment from an abundance of glorious ingredients offered to me by genial hosts at the Iron Horse Vineyard in Sonoma County, California, USA.

Serves 2

8 small button mushrooms (See Tip)

4 baby asparagus

raspberry vinegar

olive oil

4 kumquats (See Tip)

4–6 garlic cloves depending on taste

sage loaves

6 lamb loin chops

4 baby leeks

FOR THE SAUCE

juice of 2 Meyer lemons (See Tip) or 1 lemon and 1 orange

2 egg yolks

115g/4oz butter, melted

1 Marinate the mushrooms and asparagus in raspberry vinegar and olive oil for 10 minutes. Make mini-brochettes, alternating the mushrooms, kumquats, garlic cloves and sage leaves. (Brochette is the French name for a special type of skewer but you can use ordinary metal ones.)

2 Brush the lamb with oil and barbecue until charred on the outside and pink in the middle. Barbecue the marinated asparagus and leeks and the mini-brochettes.

3 Make the sauce: place the lemon or mixed fruit juices in a bowl over a pan of simmering water, add the egg yolks and whisk quickly. Add the melted butter and continue to whisk until thickened. Pour some sauce on to each plate, place the lamb on top and garnish with the young vegetables and mini-brochettes.

Nutrition notes per serving: *982 calories, Protein 42g, Carbohydrate 6g, Fat 88g, Saturated fat 47g, Fibre 2g, Added sugar trace, Salt 1.10g*

TIP

I used wonderful little golden mushrooms called cinnamon caps but you can substitute small button mushrooms. The special flavour of this dish comes from the Meyer lemons – little Californian delights which are a sort of cross between a lemon and tangerine. Sadly, unless you are planning a trip to Sonoma County, the closest you can probably get is to use a mixture of lemon and orange juice. Choose fruits that feel heavy for their size. Small, thin-skinned varieties will be juicier, larger knobbly ones will have more peel and pith in proportion to flesh. Kumquats are a close relative of the citrus fruit family, these are tiny with smooth, orange, edible skin and an unusual sour-sweet flavour. They can be eaten raw, candied and preserved.

PORK KEBABS WITH PINEAPPLE

A delightfully fruity combination.

TV Cooks **KEITH FLOYD COOKS BARBECUES**

Serves 4

675g pork fillet, cut into 2.5cm/1in thick slices

8 cocktail sausages

8 pieces canned pineapple, drained and soaked in white rum

8 stoned dried prunes, soaked in red wine for 3–4 hours

3 tbsp oil

1 tsp prepared mustard

1 tsp paprika

salt

1   Thread the pork, sausages, drained pineapple and drained prunes on to four skewers. Reserve the rum.

2   Mix together the oil, mustard, paprika and salt to a paste and paint it over the kebabs. Barbecue the kebabs for 15 minutes or until cooked. Place a drip tray, containing the remaining paste, underneath. Turn the kebabs several times and baste with the mixture from the tray.

3   Serve the kebabs with the paste and juices from the meat which will have amalgamated to make a delicious sauce. Add the rum from the pineapple to make it stretch further if you like.

Nutrition notes per serving: *468 calories, Protein 39g, Carbohydrate 9g, Fat 30g, Saturated fat 9g, Fibre trace, Added sugar none, Salt 1.16g*

TIP

If you can't be bothered with sauces or marinades buy enough fresh green and red chillies to half-fill a preserving jar, add some pickling spice and real malt vinegar. Then, when you make some simple pork kebabs, just nibble a little bit of the chilli with each mouthful. Very hot but superb.

MOROCCAN KEBABS

A bit tricky to assemble, but worth every moment.

Serves 4

12 large fresh mint leaves

2 tbsp oil

salt

550g minced lamb or beef

½ tsp cinnamon

1 tsp ground cumin

2 tsp paprika

pinch of cayenne pepper

2 tbsp finely chopped fresh parsley

1 tbsp finely chopped fresh coriander

1 large onion, finely grated

1   Keep aside the mint leaves, oil and salt, then mix everything else by hand into 12 balls.

2   Place each ball on a skewer and squeeze out until you have a sausage shape about 6cm/2½in long. You must take care to pinch the sausage on tightly so that it does not fall off during cooking. Wrap each sausage with a mint leaf.

3   Paint with oil and barbecue for 6–8 minutes, turning frequently. Sprinkle with salt just before serving.

Nutrition notes per serving: *276 calories, Protein 30g, Carbohydrate 5g, Fat 15g, Saturated fat 6g, Fibre 1g, Added sugar none, Salt 0.32g*

THE GASTRONAUT'S HAMBURGER WITH BARBECUE SAUCE ✳

A good hamburger should taste like the the sound of 'Under the Boardwalk', a great pop song from the late sixties. Anyone found using frozen hamburgers will lose the status of Honorary Gastronaut that comes free with this book.

Serves 4

675g beef, finely chopped rather than minced

1 hard-boiled egg, finely chopped

1 onion, finely chopped

1 tbsp snipped fresh chives

1 tbsp finely chopped fresh parsley

1 tbsp finely chopped fresh chervil

2 tbsp olive oil

salt and freshly ground black pepper

1 tbsp mild French mustard

fresh green salad leaves, to serve

FOR THE BARBECUE SAUCE

2 garlic cloves

½ tsp salt

½ tsp paprika

4 tbsp clear honey

3 tbsp tomato purée

4 tbsp fresh orange juice

4 tbsp white or red wine vinegar

6 tbsp dark soy sauce

1 Make the barbecue sauce: crush the garlic and salt in a pestle and mortar. Grind in the paprika, then stir in the honey and the remaining ingredients, one at a time, stirring all the while. Alternatively, you could whizz all the ingredients in a food processor. Transfer to a pan and simmer the sauce for 5–10 minutes. Serve hot or cold.

2 Place all the hamburger ingredients, apart from the mustard, in a bowl, mix very thoroughly and roll into a ball. Divide the ball into four smaller ones of equal size and with the palm of your hand flatten them to the desired thickness.

3 Before placing the hamburgers on the barbecue, spread each one with mustard. Cook over a very hot fire for 10 minutes, turning frequently until cooked right through to the centre. If the outsides are cooking too fast, move the hamburgers further away from the heat. Serve with the barbecue sauce and fresh green salad leaves.

Nutrition notes per serving: *383 calories, Protein 40g, Carbohydrate 24g, Fat 15g, Saturated fat 4g, Fibre 1g, Added sugar 15g, Salt 4.81g*

✳ *If you make up a double batch of the hamburgers you can freeze them, uncooked, for up to 1 month.*

TIP

Fresh herbs are delectable and indispensable flavourings for grills. Use them as you will, singly or mixed, but always with discretion. They should support, refine and augment the taste of the principal ingredient, not dominate or mask it. Fresh herbs are best used to enhance sauces, butters and oils. Dried herbs are superb in marinades or scattered over the fire during the cooking process.

SPICED SPARE RIBS

I love pork and these spicy ribs are a real favourite of mine.

Serves 4

1.3kg lean pork spare ribs, trimmed and chined for ease of separating after cooking

FOR THE MARINADE

4 tbsp hoisin sauce

55g/2oz sugar

1 tbsp rice wine or dry sherry

1 tbsp oyster sauce

½ tsp five-spice powder

1 Mix together the marinade ingredients. Add the spare ribs, cover, and leave for at least 4 hours.

2 Remove the ribs from the marinade and cook over medium hot coals, turning occasionally, for about 30–40 minutes until brown. Separate the ribs before serving.

Nutrition notes per serving: *522 calories, Protein 35g, Carbohydrate 2g, Fat 42g, Saturated fat 16g, Fibre trace, Added sugar 1g, Salt 0.45g*

INDIAN KEBABS

These are absolutely delicious with hot or iced mint tea, but because your guests will think you are mean if you do not offer them alcohol, why not lace the tea with crème de menthe and vodka.

Serves 4

675g shoulder of lamb, cut into cubes

FOR THE MARINADE

150ml/¼ pint coconut milk

½ tsp ground ginger

½ tsp cayenne pepper

½ tsp ground cumin

1 tsp sugar

salt and freshly ground black pepper

FOR THE SAUCE

115g/4oz peanuts or pistachios, diced

150ml/¼ pint coconut milk

2 tbsp oil

juice of ½ lemon

1 small onion, finely chopped

1 garlic clove, finely chopped

1 tsp white wine vinegar

1 tsp sugar

1 Mix together the marinade ingredients, then add the cubed lamb. Cover and and leave for 1 hour.

2 Meanwhile, make the sauce: whack all the ingredients, plus seasoning, into the merry food processor and whizz at maximum speed for 2 minutes until beautifully smooth. Pour into a sauce boat and place in the fridge.

3 Remove the lamb from the marinade, thread on to skewers and barbecue, turning frequently, for about 10 minutes or until cooked to your liking.

Nutrition notes per serving: *629 calories, Protein 39g, Carbohydrate 10g, Fat 48g, Saturated fat 18g, Fibre 2g, Added sugar 1g, Salt 0.55g*

TIP

Cumin seeds, whether crushed, whole or ground, are great with lamb and beef as well as with grilled fish such as tuna or mackerel.

FILLET STEAK WITH HORSERADISH

Fillet steak is horrifically expensive so take care with your cooking. Never prick meat while it is cooking, or you will lose valuable and delicious juices. Learn to judge its 'cookedness' by pressing it with your fingers. Be careful when preparing horseradish, it is a plant of the mustard family and difficult to handle. When you peel the knobbly root, which you must, and grate it the vapours can make your eyes water. Serve this with Pink Hollandaise sauce.

Serves 4

4 x 175g fillet steaks

FOR THE MARINADE

5 tbsp oil

4 tbsp Cognac

juice of ½ lemon

1 head horseradish, freshly grated, or 2 tbsp horseradish sauce

1 garlic clove, crushed to a paste

1 onion, finely grated

2 tsp fresh tarragon, chervil and basil, mixed together

salt and freshly ground black pepper

FOR THE GARNISH

4 cooked artichoke hearts

8 cooked asparagus spears

4 small tomatoes, halved

heart of 1 lettuce, cut into 4

150ml/¼ pint Pink Hollandaise sauce (recipe follows)

1 Mix together the marinade ingredients and coat the steaks. Leave in a covered dish for at least 30 minutes, turning the meat from time to time.

2 Remove the steaks from the marinade, then barbecue over a hot fire for 3–4 minutes on each side. During this time, place the artichoke hearts, asparagus and tomatoes on the edge of the grill to heat through. Serve the steaks with the lettuce leaves and grilled vegetables and coat with the pink hollandaise.

Nutrition notes per serving: 453 calories, Protein 38g, Carbohydrate 3g, Fat 32g, Saturated fat 17g, Fibre 1g, Added sugar none, Salt 0.60g

TIP

A well-cooked steak should be golden and crunchy on the outside, tender, juicy and warm inside – whether you like it blue, rare or well done. To achieve this perfect state you must seal the meat on all sides as quickly as possible over the hottest part of the fire. It is the sugar in the meat which caramelises and gives the desired golden, crunchy and appetising result. Of course, if the meat is thick you simply raise it further from the fire to continue the cooking process.

PINK HOLLANDAISE SAUCE

The tomato purée gives this sauce a hint of pink and it is made the quick and easy Floyd way.

350g/12oz unsalted butter

6 eggs

juice of 1 lemon

freshly ground black pepper

1 tsp tomato purée

1 Melt the butter in a pan with a pouring lip. Place the eggs, lemon juice and pepper in a food processor and turn on.

2 Pour the hot melted butter evenly into the whisking eggs until the sauce thickens. Stir in the tomato purée. To keep warm, place in a bowl over a pan of warm water until ready to serve.

Nutrition notes per rounded tablespoon: 109 calories, Protein 1g, Carbohydrate trace, Fat 12g, Saturated fat 7g, Fibre none, Added sugar none, Salt 0.02g

Poultry & Game

VENISON AND APRICOT KEBABS

Serve this with freshly cooked pasta tossed in the juices in the drip tray. You can also use this marinade for marinating beef, pork, lamb and veal. Leave the meat for two hours before cooking.

Serves 4

450g venison meat, cut into 2.5cm/1in cubes

16 dried apricots, soaked in dry sherry

16 thin rashers rindless smoked bacon

16 thin slices speck (fat bacon)

salt and freshly ground black pepper

flatleaf parsley, to garnish

tagliatelle, to serve

FOR THE BIGARADE MARINADE

grated rind of ½ orange

juice of 1 orange

grated rind of ½ lemon

1 glass Madeira

4 medium onions, grated

pinch of cayenne pepper

1 tsp freshly ground black pepper

½ tsp salt

1 Mix together the marinade ingredients, then marinate the venison cubes, covered, for at least 2 hours.

2 Remove the apricots from the sherry and reserve the soaking liquid. Wrap each apricot with smoked bacon and the venison cubes with half a slice of speck. Reserve the marinade. Thread the apricots and venison on to four skewers.

3 Place a drip tray under the kebabs together with the strained marinade and the juices from the apricots. Gently barbecue the kebabs for 15 minutes so that the bacon does not burn before the meat is cooked. Turn from time to time. Season with salt and pepper, garnish with flatleaf parsley and serve with pasta.

Nutrition notes per serving: *1049 calories, Protein 44g, Carbohydrate 38g, Fat 77g, Saturated fat 31g, Fibre 6g, Added sugar 1g, Salt 4.81g*

TIP

Low in fat and high in protein, venison is the name of all the meat from the deer family. There are four types of deer used in Britain for food. Their season depends on the breed, whether the deer is male or female and varies from one part of the country to the other. Some venison comes from parks or farms, some is wild. Venison meat is very fine-textured, dense and dark and has little fat on it and little marbling of fat in the flesh. If you do see any traces of fat, carefully remove before cooking as it will spoil the flavour of the meat. Do not overcook venison, it should be fairly pink when served.

BARBECUED CHICKEN WINGS

This dish is from Florida. It can be cooked on the barbecue or indoors in the oven if it's raining.

Serves 6

2.25kg chicken wings

salt to taste

2 tsp freshly ground black pepper

3 tsp paprika

125ml/4fl oz corn oil plus extra for brushing

250ml/9fl oz tomato ketchup

85g/3oz clear honey

1 tbsp crushed garlic

6 tbsp white wine vinegar

2 tbsp Worcestershire sauce

1 tsp Tabasco sauce

1 tsp Dijon mustard

4 tbsp butter

1 fresh bay leaf plus extra to garnish

1 Preheat the barbecue to hot or the oven to 400F/200C/Gas 6. Sprinkle the chicken wings with two teaspoons of paprika, salt and the pepper, brush over the oil, coating the wings well. Cook on the barbecue, turning, or in the oven for 15 minutes.

2 Mix together the remaining ingredients including 125ml/4 fl oz of oil and the remaining paprika and bring to the boil in a pan. Brush some of this sauce over the wings. Turn them over, and brush the other side. Return to the barbecue or oven for 15 minutes. Repeat this process twice more, until the wings have been cooked for a total of 1 hour. Serve garnished with fresh bay leaves.

Nutrition notes per serving: *466 calories, Protein 37g, Carbohydrate 3g, Fat 34g, Saturated fat 9g, Fibre trace, Added sugar 2g, Salt 0.75g*

CHICKEN BREASTS 'TWO RIVERS'

An imaginary centuries old settlement of mandarins, inhabiting an area between the River Hi Po and the Bristol Avon, would have prepared this dish for visiting colour-supplement food writers.

Serves 2

2 chicken breasts, skinned and halved
FOR THE MARINADE

2 spring onions, finely chopped

3 garlic cloves, crushed

4 tsp red bean paste

1 tbsp sesame seed oil

1 tbsp sesame seeds

1 tbsp sugar

1 tbsp dark soy sauce

freshly ground black pepper

green salad leaves, to serve

1 Flatten the chicken breasts with the flat side of a heavy knife and score the flesh. Mix together the marinade ingredients, then coat the chicken breasts all over with the marinade. Cover and leave for 1 hour.

2 Barbecue the breasts for at least 5 minutes on each side until cooked through. Serve with a crisp, green salad.

Nutrition notes per serving: *157 calories, Protein 27g, Carbohydrate 1g, Fat 5g, Saturated fat 1g, Fibre trace, Added sugar 1g, Salt 0.42g*

TIP

Red bean paste is available from larger supermarkets and Oriental food shops.

SPICED CHICKEN

On a sailing holiday once, I found myself stranded in Motril in southern Spain with no money or food. For several days I lived off dabs that I could catch in the harbour. Delicious as they were I was very pleased when a fellow sailor invited me to a beach party. Strange chap, also waiting for money to arrive, he was living on a rotting 'gun boat', the sort of thing they used to send up the Yangtze river. He was some kind of ex-patriate who, after a lifetime in Africa, found he couldn't settle in the UK and so just drifted from place to place with a Somali cook, eating the most amazingly spiced food. I ate this dish of theirs until I was fit to burst it was so good.

Serves 6

450g/1lb red peppers, seeded and sliced

115g/4oz fresh red chillies, seeded and sliced

125ml/4fl oz olive oil

juice of 1 lemon

salt

1 x 1.3–1.8kg chicken, jointed

green salad, to serve

1 Cook the peppers and chillies in a pan of boiling, salted water until tender, then purée in a blender or food processor. Stir in the olive oil and lemon juice and add salt as necessary, then leave to cool.
2 When cold, rub the spicy sauce all over the chicken joints. Cover the dish and place in the fridge overnight.
3 Barbecue the chicken pieces for about 40 minutes, or until cooked through, turning from time to time. Serve with a green salad.

Nutrition notes per serving: *335 calories, Protein 24g, Carbohydrate 1g, Fat 26g, Saturated fat 7g, Fibre trace, Added sugar none, Salt 0.41g*

CHICKEN KEBABS WITH OREGANO

Serve this with saffron rice (See Tip) and a piquant sauce of your choice (See pages 56–9).

Serves 4

4 chicken breasts, cut into cubes

1 slice thick ham, cut into cubes

1 red pepper, cut into cubes

FOR THE MARINADE

juice of 1 lemon

3 tbsp oil

1 garlic clove, crushed

1 tsp dried oregano

salt and freshly ground black pepper

coriander, to garnish

1 Mix together the marinade ingredients, add the chicken and ham. Cover and leave for at least 1 hour.
2 Thread the chicken, ham and red pepper on to skewers and barbecue for about 8 minutes, basting from time to time with the marinade, until the chicken is cooked. Serve garnished with coriander.

Nutrition notes per serving: *319 calories, Protein 24g, Carbohydrate 2g, Fat 24g, Saturated fat 7g, Fibre 1g, Added sugar none, Salt 0.67g*

TIP

Saffron, the dried stigmas of the purple-flowering saffron crocus, is one of the world's most expensive spices. Now imported mostly from Spain, it has an aromatic, slightly bitter taste and only a few threads are needed to flavour and colour dishes. The threads should be infused in a little hot liquid, then stirred into the rice. Powdered saffron is also available. Where just a touch of colour is needed you can use a pinch of turmeric instead, but the flavour is not the same.

GRILLED POUSSINS WITH MUSTARD

Poussins, also known as spring chickens, are aged 4–6 weeks old and weigh 350–450g. They are often tasteless when cooked in the normal way. Charcoal grilling really improves their flavour.

Serves 6

3 poussins

oil

salt

25g/1oz butter

1 tsp mustard

dried fresh white breadcrumbs

1 Clean the poussins and split them in half lengthways, crushing them with a heavy knife and breaking the bones so that they lie flat while cooking.

2 Brush the poussins with oil and sprinkle with salt. Cook for about 10 minutes on each side on the barbecue.

3 Make a paste with the butter and mustard. Spread the paste over the cooked poussins and sprinkle with breadcrumbs. Return to the barbecue and cook until golden brown.

Nutrition notes per serving: *486 calories, Protein 31g, Carbohydrate 52g, Fat 19g, Saturated fat 7g, Fibre 1g, Added sugar none, Salt 1.71g*

CHICKEN AND VEGETABLE KEBABS

To my mind the average frozen chicken is tasteless. If you are not lucky enough to have free-range ones pecking about the bottom of the garden, look carefully around the supermarkets for one that sells imported French maize-fed birds, recognisable by their yellow skin. They are a little more expensive than the ubiquitous unidentified clucking object, but for taste they are much superior and well worth the extra you pay.

Serves 6

1 x 1.3kg chicken, cut into small pieces

6 chicken livers, halved or quartered

4 leeks, white parts only, cut into 2.5cm/1in pieces

1 onion, coarsely chopped to go on a skewer

2 green peppers, seeded and cut into small pieces

1 garlic clove, finely chopped

115ml/4fl oz light soy sauce

4 tbsp dry sherry

4 tbsp sake (See Tip)

2 tsp sugar

¼ tsp cayenne pepper

2.5cm/1in piece of fresh root ginger, finely chopped

1 Starting and ending with the chicken arrange two chicken pieces, then one piece each of liver, leek, onion and pepper on to oiled skewers.

2 Place the garlic, soy sauce, sherry, sake, sugar, cayenne pepper and ginger in a pan and bring to the boil. Pour over the skewered chicken and leave to marinate, covered, for about 1 hour.

3 Barbecue the kebabs for 2–3 minutes, turning regularly. Dip the skewers back into the marinade, then barbecue for at least another 5 minutes or until the chicken is cooked.

Nutrition notes per serving: *375 calories, Protein 30g, Carbohydrate 5g, Fat 26g, Saturated fat 8g, Fibre 2g, Added sugar trace, Salt 0.58g*

TIP

Sake, or mirin as it is also known, is a Japanese fermented colourless sweet rice wine. If you can't find it use sweet sherry or Madeira.

GRILLED QUAILS

A delicious treat. Quails are now being cultivated as domesticated birds on farms and are available oven-ready, fresh or frozen, all year round.

Serves 4

4 plump quails

4 fresh thyme sprigs

4 small knobs butter

4 long slices speck (fat bacon)

salt and freshly ground black pepper

4 croûtons of lightly toasted bread, spread with butter and anchovy paste

fresh basil and thyme, to garnish

1 You will need a fairly gentle fire for cooking this dish. Rub the salt and pepper inside each quail, then push in a thyme sprig and a knob of butter.

2 Wrap each quail carefully and tightly with a strip of speck. Thread on to a skewer and roast gently, turning frequently for at least 30 minutes.

3 Just before serving, lift the quails off the fire, discard the speck and place them on the croûtons so that the last drops of fat are absorbed. Serve garnished with fresh basil and thyme.

Nutrition notes per serving: *462 calories, Protein 36g, Carbohydrate 11g, Fat 30g, Saturated fat 10g, Fibre trace, Added sugar none, Salt 1.97g*

TIP

Whenever you are roasting poultry ensure that you have a drip tray underneath, because to get the skin crisp all round it must be basted frequently. There is no harm in putting a little alcohol into the drip tray along with a few herbs, thus enhancing the cooking juices.

VENISON CHOPS WITH BACON

If you are lucky enough to live next door to my mother you would have spent the morning raiding her chestnut tree and preparing a purée of chestnuts to go with these delicious game chops. However, if you are unable to obtain fresh chestnuts, a purée of canned chick peas with lots of pepper and melted butter will make a supreme accompaniment.

Serves 4

8 venison chops

8 slices rindless smoked bacon

FOR THE MARINADE

4 tbsp oil

juice of 1 lemon

1 tbsp Worcestershire sauce

salt and freshly ground black pepper

fresh herbs, to garnish

1 Mix together the marinade ingredients and marinate the chops for 1 hour.

2 Simply barbecue the chops for 5 minutes on each side and just before they are cooked, barbecue the bacon for a minute or two on each side. Serve garnished with a selection of fresh herbs.

Nutrition notes per serving: *404 calories, Protein 52g, Carbohydrate trace, Fat 22g, Saturated fat 8g, Fibre none, Added sugar none, Salt 1.86g*

Fish & Shellfish

GRILLED MACKEREL

Fennel has a beautiful flavour of aniseed which goes very well with grilled fish.

Serves 4

4 whole mackerel, cleaned

juice of 1 lemon

salt

4 tbsp mixed chopped fresh fennel leaves, parsley, thyme and chervil

1–2 garlic cloves, finely chopped

125ml/4fl oz oil

fresh herbs, to serve

1 Slash the mackerel on each side with a sharp knife and sprinkle the inside and outside with some of the lemon juice and salt. Stuff the herbs and some of the garlic into each fish.

2 Mix the remaining garlic, lemon juice and oil together. Barbecue the fish for at least 5 minutes on each side until tender, basting with the lemon and oil mixture. Serve garnished with fresh herbs.

Nutrition notes per serving: *464 calories, Protein 39g, Carbohydrate 1g, Fat 34g, Saturated fat 8g, Fibre 1g, Added sugar none, Salt 0.92g*

TIP

Fish in general should be undercooked rather than overcooked, though the skin should be crisp. The flesh should separate from the bones easily but without crumbling.

FISH PARCELS

A simple and delicious way to cook any white fish fillet.

Serves 8

8 white fish fillets

115g/4oz onions, finely chopped

115g/4oz mushrooms, finely chopped

25g/1oz capers

55g/2oz butter

300ml/½ pint single cream

chopped fresh parsley, to serve

baby spinach, to serve

1 Grease eight large pieces of double-thickness buttered foil. Pop a fillet on to each piece of foil, then divide the remaining ingredients, except the parsley, and place on and around each fillet.

2 Wrap the foil loosely to make parcels and cook on the barbecue for 25–30 minutes or until the fish is cooked. Sprinkle with parsley and the fish juices and serve with baby spinach.

Nutrition notes per serving: *268 calories, Protein 32g, Carbohydrate 3g, Fat 14g, Saturated fat 8g, Fibre 1g, Added sugar trace, Salt 0.55g*

SWEET AND SOUR BREAM KEBABS

Bream is a fine, delicate fish easily found in Britain, but, of course, little used. It is highly esteemed in France and Spain. Two varieties are available here, the black bream and the red. The red bream makes better eating. You can substitute any firm-fleshed white fish if you prefer.

Serves 4

900g/2lb bream fillets, cut into 4cm/1½in square slices

8 cherry tomatoes, halved

16 small onions, halved

FOR THE MARINADE

juice of 2 lemons

1 garlic clove, crushed

2 pinches of salt

FOR THE BASTING LIQUID

4 tbsp oil

2 tbsp sherry

½ tsp sugar

salt and freshly ground black pepper

FOR THE SAUCE

1 tbsp roughly chopped fresh parsley

1 tsp snipped fresh chives

1 small tub natural yogurt

125ml/4fl oz double cream

juice of ½ lemon

salt

1 Mix together the marinade ingredients and marinate the fish pieces for about 15 minutes. Mix together the basting ingredients.

2 Remove the fish from the marinade and thread eight skewers alternately with fish, tomatoes and onions. Paint with the basting liquid. Barbecue the kebabs for 10 minutes, turning and basting often.

3 While the kebabs are cooking, mix together the sauce ingredients, place in a bowl and serve with the kebabs.

Nutrition notes per serving: *413 calories, Protein 43g, Carbohydrate 11g, Fat 22g, Saturated fat 10g, Fibre 2g, Added sugar trace, Salt 0.69g*

TIP

Ignore unidentified frozen objects in freezer cabinets and make friends with a fishmonger. Buy only the freshest fish. Fish from the sea should smell of sea water not of fish. And don't be afraid to prod and poke the fish before you buy it – it should be firm and tight, not soggy or flaky. If buying whole fish, the eyes should be bright, almost alert, and the gills bright red. Fillets should be firm and moist and white fish should be a good white colour with no discolouration or signs of dryness.

MACKEREL FILLETS BAKED IN FOIL ENVELOPES

This recipe can be applied to any filleted fish you like.

Serves 4

4 tsp butter

4 large mackerel fillets

juice of 1 lime

salt and freshly ground black pepper

4 small bay leaves (See Tip)

4 small fresh parsley sprigs

4 thin lemon slices

1 heaped tsp capers

4 tbsp single cream

1 Butter four rectangles of foil and place a fillet on each one. Brush each fillet with lime juice and sprinkle with salt and pepper. Place a bay leaf, parsley sprig and a slice of lemon on each fillet.

2 Divide the capers between the four fillets, fold up the foil edges and anoint each fillet with one tablespoon of cream.

3 Close the envelopes and place them near the edge of the fire for 10 minutes or until the fillets are cooked. Open carefully to avoid spilling any juices and munch away.

Nutrition notes per serving: *517 calories, Protein 39g, Carbohydrate 1g, Fat 40g, Saturated fat 12g, Fibre trace, Added sugar trace, Salt 1.04g*

TIP

Bay leaves are indispensable in stews and casseroles and vital to many marinades. They are also good to throw on the coals since they release a wonderful aroma which will subtly flavour the dish that you are cooking. They are especially good with oily fish such as mackerel.

GRILLED SARDINES, SPRATS, ANCHOVIES OR ANY SMALL FISH

Aficionados do not gut sardines. They dry them carefully, paint with herb grilling oil and pop them on to a hot grill for 3–4 minutes each side. You should clean and bone anchovies, sprats and pilchards if using.

FOR THE HERB GRILLING OIL

30 black peppercorns

6 bay leaves

3 fresh rosemary sprigs

4 fresh thyme sprigs

4 fresh red chillies

4–5 fresh sage leaves

½ tsp fennel seeds

20 coriander seeds

best quality olive oil

1 Stuff all the dry ingredients into a 1 litre/1¾ pint bottle. Cover with the olive oil and whack in the cork or screw on the top.

2 Leave for a week or two to use as and when you wish.

Nutrition notes per serving of one sardine: *197 calories, Protein 29g, Carbohydrate none, Fat 9g, Saturated fat 2g, Fibre none, Added sugar none, Salt 0.38g*

RED MULLET PARCELS

In Spain and around the Mediterranean generally, small red mullet are grilled with their intestines and considered a great delicacy. In France, they tend to remove the guts but leave the liver, which is highly prized. As a general rule, red mullet are fried or grilled. They do not lend themselves to poaching. As with grey mullet, the red mullet must be carefully scaled (See Tip).

Serves 6

12 small red mullet

12 thin rindless rashers lean bacon

6 fresh bay leaves, halved

salt and freshly ground black pepper

FOR THE AIOLI

8 garlic cloves

2 egg yolks

juice of 1 lemon

salt and freshly ground black pepper

400ml/14fl oz best olive oil

1   Make the aioli: place all the ingredients, except the olive oil, in a food processor, turn on and process for a few seconds to crush the garlic, then pour in the oil slowly but evenly, until you have a beautiful thick sauce.

2   Season the fish, then wrap a piece of bacon around each fish and secure with a cocktail stick. Insert a bay leaf half between the bacon and the fish.

3   Barbecue the fish, turning regularly, for 10 minutes or until cooked. Remove the bay leaves and the cocktail sticks and serve with a bowl of wobbling aioli, a green salad.

Nutrition notes per serving: *925 calories, Protein 59g, Carbohydrate 1g, Fat 74g, Saturated fat xg, Fibre trace, Added sugar none, Salt 2.60g*

TIP

If you just want to simply barbecue whole red mullet, leave the scales on and the liver inside and brush the fish inside and out with Herb grilling oil (See page 39).

SHELLFISH AND GRAPE KEBABS Ⓕ

Naturally you can use any combination of fish or shellfish to make this extremely simple and delightful kebab. The important thing is that the fish should be very fresh.

Serves 4

12 cooked langoustine tails

12 cooked large peeled prawns

12 large mussels, cooked and shelled

large cucumber, cut into 1cm/½in thick slices

115g/4oz seedless black grapes

115g/4oz seedless white grapes

sunflower oil

1   Thread the shellfish, cucumber and grapes attractively on to eight metal or wooden skewers.

2   Brush with oil and barbecue for about 4 minutes on each side or until completely warmed through.

Nutrition notes per serving: *188 calories, Protein 32g, Carbohydrate 11g, Fat 2g, Saturated fat trace, Fibre trace, Added sugar none, Salt 2.92*

GRILLED SEAFOOD

This recipe was given to me by Rick Stein of *The Seafood Restaurant*, Padstow, while I was researching my book and television series *Floyd on Britain and Ireland*.

Serves 4–6

2 x 450g/1lb cooked lobsters, cut in half lengthways and claws cracked

24 cooked Dublin Bay prawns

4 x 115g/4oz monkfish steaks

4 x 85g/3oz grey mullet steaks

lemon wedges, to serve

FOR THE MARINADE

50ml/2fl oz olive oil

1 tsp chopped fresh fennel

3 fresh bay leaves, cut into pieces

salt and freshly ground black pepper

juice of ¼ lemon

FOR THE FENNEL DRESSING

150ml/¼ pint olive oil

30ml/1fl oz red wine vinegar

½ tsp salt

freshly ground black pepper

1 tbsp chopped fresh fennel

½ small onion, finely chopped

1 Mix together all the dressing ingredients. Prepare and light your barbecue at least 40 minutes before cooking begins.

2 At least 1 hour before cooking, place all the marinade ingredients in a shallow dish and add the fish steaks. Turn over in the marinade two or three times during the hour. Reserve the marinade and remove the fish.

3 Cook the fish steaks for about 3 minutes on each side. The lobsters and prawns, being cooked already, don't need to go on the barbecue for very long: they should just be warmed through. This also lightly chars the shells, giving the grillade a spectacular aroma which is one of the best attractions of the dish.

4 Brush the lobster and prawn shells with some of the marinade you used for the fish and place the lobsters on the barbecue for about 2 minutes per side; prawns for about 1 minute.

5 Serve everything on one large serving dish. Add any of the marinade left to the dressing and pour over the cooked fish. Serve with lemon wedges and plenty of French bread to mop up the dressing.

Nutrition notes per serving: *743 calories, Protein 63g, Carbohydrate 2g, Fat 54g, Saturated fat 8g, Fibre trace, Added sugar trace, Salt 2.04g*

TIP

In this recipe you can use 12 Mediterranean prawns or 36 North Atlantic prawns instead of the Dublin Bay variety. You can also substitute quite a few other types of fish for the grey mullet – steaks of conger eel, dogfish, tope or shark; or whole small mackerel, red mullet, sardines, pilchards, black breams, small John Dory, gurnard or sea bass.

MARINATED FISH WITH YOGURT AND SPICES

With the profusion of signs saying 'Last trout farm before the motorway' the trout, that wonderful fine-fleshed fish of my youth, has become something of a gastronomic joke. And trout with almonds is clichéd beyond belief. What was a few years ago a treat has today become the lazy restaurateur's token 'fish dish'. If you are to eat trout simply, say grilled or fried in butter, the farmed trout does need plenty of seasoning by way of salt and pepper and lemon juice, inside and out, and be sure to use a very hot grill so that the skin chars a bit. This tasty marinated dish is delicious served with iced lager, warm naan bread and a fine lime pickle.

Serves 6

6 trout, cleaned (See Tip)

melted butter, for basting

FOR THE MARINADE

½ tsp paprika

4 tbsp coriander seeds

½ tsp salt

6 cardamom seeds

2 onions, finely chopped

2 garlic cloves

¼ tsp freshly ground black pepper

1 tbsp chopped fresh dill, plus extra to garnish

½ green pepper, seeded

2 tbsp chopped fresh mint

juice of 1 lemon

175ml/6fl oz natural yogurt

1 Place all the marinade ingredients, except the yogurt, in a food processor, or pestle and mortar if you are feeling energetic. Whizz or grind until you have a paste, then stir into the yogurt.

2 Spread the paste over and inside the trout and leave to marinate, covered, for 1 hour. Remove the fish from the marinade and reserve the marinade.

3 Grill the trout over a barbecue until they are cooked and crisp. During cooking, turn the fish from time to time, and baste with butter and the reserved marinade. Garnish with fresh dill sprigs.

Nutrition notes per serving: *246 calories, Protein 32g, Carbohydrate 8g, Fat 10g, Saturated fat 3g, Fibre 1g, Added sugar none, Salt 0.81g*

TIP

Instead of trout, you can use whiting or perch, or thick fillets of white fish such as hake or cod. Grill whole fish whenever possible with their scales on. This forms a kind of envelope around the fish and enables the juices to stay inside. In any event, if you have grilled your fish golden and crunchy as you should, the scales will have burnt away leaving just the crisp skin.

BROCHETTES OF SCALLOPS WITH BACON

Have your fishmonger remove the scallops from their shells if you don't fancy the task.

Serves 4

24 large scallops (See Tip)

1 tsp fresh oregano

freshly ground black pepper

24 thin slices rindless unsmoked bacon

55g/2oz butter

juice of 1 lemon

1 Sprinkle the scallops with oregano and pepper and wrap them carefully in bacon. Thread on to four skewers.

2 Place a drip tray under the grill to catch the juices and barbecue the brochettes, turning frequently until the bacon is lightly crisped.

3 The scallops should be firm but slightly undercooked and moist. Whisk the juices from the drip tray with the butter and lemon juice and pour over the scallops to serve.

Nutrition notes per serving: *581 calories, Protein 46g, Carbohydrate trace, Fat 44g, Saturated fat 20g, Fibre trace, Added sugar none, Salt 4.09g*

TIP

There are two basic scallops: the great scallop, usually about 13cm/5in in diameter and supreme for gourmandising, and the smaller but tasty queen scallop, which I like to use for less sophisticated meals. Some people steam scallops open in the oven, but this inevitably starts to cook them, which is not to be encouraged, although it is easier than prising them open.

GRILLED RED MULLET

Red mullet imported from around India are not so good as the Mediterranean or British ones. Ask where they come from before buying.

Serves 2

4 red mullets, cleaned

fresh thyme sprigs

fresh fennel fronds

olive oil

salt and freshly ground black pepper

1 Stuff the fish cavities with the thyme and fennel fronds.

2 Barbecue the fish over very hot coals, basting constantly with olive oil. They will take about 10 minutes each side. Sprinkle with salt and pepper before serving.

Nutrition notes per serving: *319 calories, Protein 50g, Carbohydrate trace, Fat 12g, Saturated fat 4g, Fibre trace, Added sugar none, Salt 0.85g*

Vegetables & Salads

STUFFED MUSHROOMS Ⓥ

These are no ordinary mushrooms. They can be stuffed in advance and then just popped on to the barbecue when you need them.

Serves 4

24 large mushroom caps

125ml/4fl oz olive oil
plus 2 tbsp for frying

3 tbsp fresh lemon juice

1 red pepper, seeded and finely chopped

5 garlic cloves, finely chopped

6 shallots, finely chopped

25g/1oz fresh parsley, finely chopped

85g/3oz fresh white breadcrumbs

salt and freshly ground black pepper

flatleaf parsley, to garnish

1 Marinate the mushroom caps in 125ml/4fl oz of olive oil and the lemon juice for at least 2 hours. Drain and reserve the marinade.

2 Heat the remaining olive oil in a frying pan and sauté the pepper, garlic and shallots for 5 minutes or until they are soft.

3 Remove the pan from the heat and add the parsley and four tablespoons of the reserved marinade, then stir in the breadcrumbs. Season to taste and stuff the mushroom caps with the mixture. Barbecue for 8–10 minutes until they are well heated through. Serve garnished with flatleaf parsley.

Nutrition notes per serving: *244 calories, Protein 6g, Carbohydrate 21g, Fat 16g, Saturated fat 2g, Fibre 3g, Added sugar none, Salt 0.69g*

A VEGETABLE RAINBOW Ⓥ

A myriad of colour and taste, this dish is an attractive accompaniment to barbecued meat.

Serves 4

1 red pepper, cut in quarters lengthways

1 green pepper, cut in quarters lengthways

2 aubergines, cut lengthways in 2cm/¾in thick slices

2 large tomatoes

olive oil

salt and freshly ground black pepper

fresh basil, to garnish

1 Paint the vegetables liberally with oil, season with pepper and cook for about 10 minutes, turning and oiling all the while.

2 Once the vegetables are tender to the touch they are tender to the tongue, so remove from the barbecue and serve sprinkled with salt, a final splash of olive oil and a garnish of basil.

Nutrition notes per serving: *197 calories, Protein 3g, Carbohydrate 10g, Fat 16g, Saturated fat 2g, Fibre 6g, Added sugar none, Salt 0.28g*

TIP

Try the delights of grilled red peppers or tomatoes stuffed with chopped fresh herbs, basted with olive oil and baked under Barbecued chicken wings (page 27).

GRILLED AUBERGINES Ⓥ

A brilliant and simple way to eat aubergines, ideal for dining outdoors.

Serves 1–2

1 medium aubergine

olive oil

salt and freshly ground black pepper

1 Barbecue the aubergine, whole and unpeeled, for about 20 minutes, turning from time to time until the skin is black and it is soft and squidgy.

2 Cut the aubergine in half and, with a teaspoon, mash in olive oil to taste, salt and pepper. Spoon out the flesh rather as you would that of an avocado pear.

Nutrition notes per serving for one: *225 calories, Protein 5g, Carbohydrate 13g, Fat 17g, Saturated fat 2g, Fibre 12g, Added sugar none, Salt 1.02g*

SALSA RANCHERA Ⓥ Ⓕ

This spicy Mexican dish can also be served as an appetiser with crispy corn or tortilla chips.

Serves 4–6

5 small green chillies, seeded

pinch of salt

150ml/¼pt white wine vinegar

450g/1lb tomatoes, skinned and very finely chopped

1 In a food processor, lightly blend the chillies, salt, vinegar and 75ml/2½fl oz of water until mixed together.

2 Mix with the chopped tomatoes and chill until needed.

Nutrition notes per serving: *22 calories, Protein 1g, Carbohydrate 4g, Fat trace, Saturated fat trace, Fibre 1g, Added sugar trace, Salt 0.29g*

GRILLED SWEETCORN Ⓥ

Until I discovered this recipe I had never enjoyed fresh corn on the cob. I am sorry to say that I always thought canned corn was the best. But now my life has changed.

Serves 4

4 young fresh yellow cobs

300ml/½ pint milk

melted butter, for basting and to serve

crushed sea salt, to serve

parsley, to garnish

1 Simmer the corn cobs in milk for 15 minutes. Remove from the milk and paint with melted butter.

2 Barbecue for about 30 minutes, turning and basting with butter until the cobs are golden. Garnish with parsley and eat with the sea salt and more melted butter.

Nutrition notes per serving: *264 calories, Protein 5g, Carbohydrate 16g, Fat 21g, Saturated fat 12g, Fibre 1g, Added sugar none, Salt 0.49g*

TOMATO AND CHEESE SALAD

This will only work brilliantly if you really do use best-quality ingredients – it will be grim if you use corn oil and Cheddar cheese, for example.

Serves 6

900g/2lb tomatoes, some very ripe, some a little green, thinly sliced

1 tbsp caster sugar

sea salt and freshly ground black pepper

1 wine glass olive oil

couple of dashes white wine vinegar

4 tbsp torn fresh basil leaves

175g/6oz mozzarella cheese, cut into 5mm/¼in cubes

1 Place all the ingredients in a large salad bowl. Mix carefully so that you don't damage the tomatoes.
2 Chill for at least 1 hour and toss gently again before serving.

Nutrition notes per serving: *223 calories, Protein 7g, Carbohydrate 7g, Fat 19g, Saturated fat 5g, Fibre 1g, Added sugar 2g, Salt 0.56g*

BITTER SALAD ⓥ

This makes a delightful combination of flavours and textures when served with Brochettes of scallops with bacon (page 47).

Serves 4

55g/2oz lamb's lettuce

25g/1oz nasturtium leaves

1 escarole (broad-leaved endive) heart

55g/2oz radicchio

2 cooked artichoke hearts, sliced

olive oil

fresh lemon juice

salt and freshly ground black pepper

1 Place the lamb's lettuce, nasturtium leaves, escarole heart, radicchio and artichoke hearts together in a salad bowl.
2 Toss with oil, lemon juice and seasoning to taste. There should be plenty of lemon juice in the dressing.

Nutrition notes per serving: *68 calories, Protein 1g, Carbohydrate 1g, Fat 6g, Saturated fat 1g, Fibre 1g, Added sugar none, Salt 0.26g*

TIP

Lamb's lettuce is not a true lettuce but originally a weed native to most of Europe. It has been cultivated largely in France and Italy as a winter salad vegetable, although today it is available all year round. It is quite expensive but a little goes a long way. If you grow nasturtiums the leaves are a useful addition to the salad bowl. They have a peppery flavour not dissimilar to watercress. Don't confuse radicchio with red-leaved lettuces, it is the general Italian name for chicory. In Britain it is applied to the red, round-headed compact types. Escarole is the least bitter member of the chicory family and grows in a loose-leaved head rather like a lettuce. The leaves are bright green on the outside – some varieties are tinged red – and are pale yellow in the centre.

PROVENÇAL SALAD

A personal favourite of mine from Provence.

Serves 4

2 pale green crisp frisée

3–4 crunchy white endives, leaves left on

6 whole salted anchovies, rinsed and dried

900g/2lb tomatoes, some green, some ripe, quartered

handful pitted black olives

1 wine glass best-quality olive oil

2–3 garlic cloves, finely crushed

sea salt and freshly ground

black pepper

dash or two of white wine vinegar

4 hard-boiled free-range eggs, quartered

1 Gently combine all the ingredients, except the eggs, with your fingers in a large salad bowl.

2 Add the eggs and fluff the heavier ingredients to the top of the bowl.

Nutrition notes per serving: *391 calories, Protein 10g, Carbohydrate 8g, Fat 36g, Saturated fat 6g, Fibre 4g, Added sugar none, Salt 1.15g*

SALAD OF ENDIVE LETTUCE WITH CORIANDER DRESSING

This recipe was given to me by Shaun Hill when he was at *Gidleigh Park Hotel*, Chagford, Devon, and while I was researching my television series and book *Floyd on Britain and Ireland*. It marries superbly with the Grilled red mullet (page 47).

Serves 2–4

150ml/¼ pint olive oil

2 garlic cloves

2 fresh thyme sprigs (See Tip)

1 tbsp coriander seeds, cracked

4 firm ripe tomatoes, skinned, seeded and diced

salt and freshly ground black pepper

1 small endive lettuce, leaves separated

1 Make the dressing: warm the olive oil with the garlic cloves, thyme and coriander seeds.

2 Allow to cool, then remove the garlic and add the diced tomatoes. Season with black pepper and a little salt. Spoon the dressing over a bed of lettuce leaves and serve.

Nutrition notes per serving for two: *660 calories, Protein 3g, Carbohydrate 8g, Fat 69g, Saturated fat 10g, Fibre 3g, Added sugar none, Salt 0.05g*

TIP

Thyme is one of the most useful of herbs. It goes well with almost everything, but it must be used discreetly. And don't forget it is stronger dried than fresh. Mixed with bay leaves, savory, nutmeg and lavender it becomes that delicious mixture known as *herbes de Provence*.

Essential Extras

FLOYD'S DESERT ISLAND LIME SAUCE Ⓥ

While in Florida I made this tangy sauce to go with a grouper I caught and later barbecued over an open fire on a desert island. This goes well with any white fish.

Serves 3–4

1 tbsp olive oil

55g/2oz butter, plus a knob

55g/2oz shallots, finely chopped

55g/2oz plain flour

1½ glasses white wine

juice and grated rind of 2 limes

salt and freshly ground black pepper

1 Heat the olive oil and 55g/2oz of butter in a pan. Add the shallots and fry gently until soft. Stir in the flour to make a roux, then add the wine, followed by the lime juice, and cook, stirring, until thickened. Simmer for 4 minutes.

2 Beat in the knob of butter, stir in the grated rind and season to taste. Spoon over the fish of your choice.

Nutrition notes per serving for three: *292 calories, Protein 2g, Carbohydrate 17g, Fat 20g, Saturated fat 11g, Fibre 1g, Added sugar none, Salt 0.75g*

JAPANESE MARINADE Ⓥ ⓕ

This is a very good marinade for pork, chicken and chicken liver kebabs.

6 tbsp sake or sweet sherry or Madeira

6 tbsp dark soy sauce

1 tsp grated fresh root ginger

1 tsp dark muscovado sugar

1 garlic clove, crushed

1 Mix together all the ingredients. Marinate your meat, covered, in the fridge for at least 6 hours.

2 Dry the meat before cooking. Once sealed, baste it with the remaining marinade.

Nutrition notes: *207 calories, Protein 9g, Carbohydrate 20g, Fat trace, Saturated fat none, Fibre trace, Added sugar 11g, Salt 13.11g*

SHRIMP OR PRAWN BUTTER

This will cheer up the simplest barbecued fish.

55g/2oz cooked prawns or shrimps in their shells

dash of anchovy essence

juice of 1 lemon

150g/5½oz unsalted butter, softened

1 Grind the prawns or shrimps in a food processor. Add the remaining ingredients and whizz until smooth.

2 Roll the butter into a sausage shape, wrap in greaseproof paper or foil and pop in the fridge or freezer for use as and when desired.

Nutrition notes per 25g/1oz: *127 calories, Protein 1g, Carbohydrate trace, Fat 14g, Saturated fat 9g, Fibre none, Added sugar none, Salt 0.12g*

FLOYD'S TEXAS BARBECUE SAUCE

This is good with barbecued steak or any other meat.

Serves 4–6

1 onion, finely chopped

1 garlic clove, crushed

115g/4oz butter

1 tbsp sugar

2 tsp musard powder

2 tsp chilli powder

250ml/9fl oz tomato ketchup

125ml/4fl oz white wine vinegar

1 tbsp Worcestershire sauce

1 In a large frying pan, sauté the onion and garlic gently in the butter. Combine all the other ingredients in a bowl with 125ml/4fl oz of water, then add to the pan.

2 Bring to the boil and simmer for 5 minutes or until the sauce thickens.

Nutrition notes per serving: *324 calories, Protein 3g, Carbohydrate 23g, Fat 25g, Saturated fat 15g, Fibre 1g, Added sugar 12g, Salt 2.41g*

MAITRE D'HÔTEL BUTTER

Delicious with barbecued meat or fish.

225g/8oz unsalted butter, softened

4-5 tbsp finely chopped fresh parsley

juice of 1-2 lemons

1 Whizz all the ingredients in a food processor until smooth.

2 Roll the butter into a sausage shape, wrap in greaseproof paper or foil and pop in the fridge or freezer for use as and when desired.

Nutrition notes per 25g/1oz: *141 calories, Protein trace, Carbohydrate trace, Fat 15g, Saturated fat 10g, Fibre trace, Added sugar none, Salt 0.01g*

INSTANT MARINADE ⓕ

This is jolly useful for a spur-of-the-moment barbecue.

6 shallots, grated

1 tsp fresh rosemary spikes

1 tsp fresh thyme leaves

salt and freshly ground black pepper

150ml/¼ pint cider vinegar

1 Mix together all the ingredients and marinate your meat for 10 minutes on each side before barbecuing.

Nutrition notes: *34 calories, Protein 2g, Carbohydrate 6g, Fat trace, Saturated fat none, Fibre 2g, Added sugar trace, Salt 1.10g*

Desserts

CARAMELISED BANANAS Ⓥ Ⓕ

I could go on forever extolling the virtues of these delightful fruit kebabs. What better way to pass a summer's evening than cooking dozens of these delights while drinking exotic cocktails and swapping pompous stories with your neighbours? However, on with the bananas.

Serves 4

4 bananas, not too ripe

115g/4oz vanilla sugar (See Tip)

½ tsp ground cinnamon

large slug of whisky, Cognac or rum

1 Roll the bananas firmly in a mixture of the vanilla sugar and cinnamon. Pop them on to the grill for 2 or more minutes until they are caramelised.

2 Place them in an ovenproof serving dish. Heat the whisky, Cognac or rum in small pan and gently warm until it begins to simmer. Tilt the pan and, using a large cook's match, carefully ignite the alcohol and pour over the bananas.

Nutrition notes per serving: *221 calories, Protein 1g, Carbohydrate 54g, Fat trace, Saturated fat trace, Fibre 1g, Added sugar 30g, Salt none*

TIP

To make vanilla sugar: place two or three vanilla pods in a large jar of caster sugar and use when required. Topped up with sugar, the vanilla flavour will last for up to a year.

FRUIT KEBABS Ⓥ Ⓕ

Obviously you could pour cream over these but to my mind this perfect drink on a stick, the very essence of summer, needs no further garnish.

Serves 4

4 fresh peaches, halved and stoned

4 fresh apricots, halved and stoned

12 stoned black cherries

large glass of apricot liqueur (or any other fruit liqueur)

115g/4oz caster sugar

1 Don't peel the fruit, but wash and dry it and place it to macerate in the liqueur for 10 minutes. Drain the fruit and don't throw the liqueur away – don't drink it either; you'll need it in a minute.

2 Prepare the kebabs by threading each of four skewers with two peach halves, two apricot halves and three cherries. Sprinkle liberally with sugar and pop the kebabs on the barbecue for 5–8 minutes or until they are beautifully caramelised.

3 Place them on an ovenproof serving dish, heat the liqueur you've kept so carefully, pour it over the kebabs and set fire to it.

Nutrition notes per serving: *212 calories, Protein 2g, Carbohydrate 48g, Fat trace, Saturated fat none, Fibre 3g, Added sugar 34g, Salt 0.01g*

Barbecue Basics

Barbecuing is fun! That is the first thing that should be said, and said firmly. Of course it is important to grasp the essentials of the techniques involved, but not at the expense of the pleasure. What follows is a simple straightforward guide with tips to help you along your way. See also the Equipment Glossary on pages 6–7.

LIGHTING THE FIRE

The type of method used to ignite the fire depends very much on personal preference. Efficient methods include solid fire lighters, jellied alcohol and gas lighters operating off butane.

Build a pyramid of charcoal. When the charcoal becomes covered in ash, spread it evenly over the grate. The intensity of the heat can be varied either by separating the charcoal (to lower the intensity) or by pushing the charcoal together (to raise it).

Before you start to grill make sure that there are no flames and that the cinders are covered in fine white dust. This is when the fire is at its hottest and your meat will seal without scorching, your fat will not run and sausages won't explode.

If you can add some vine twigs, roots or pine cones to your charcoal, then so much the better. And from time to time while cooking sprinkle herbs such as basil, rosemary and thyme on to the embers. Always ensure that your chosen apparatus is hot well in advance of cooking.

GETTING THE BEST RESULTS

- Please don't follow to the letter the times that I give for cooking. Obviously they will vary depending upon the thickness of the meat and fish and the intensity of the heat.
- Make sure food is taken out of the fridge at least 1 hour before you plan to cook.
- When grilling more than one chop or steak ensure that they are cut to a uniform size so that they cook evenly and together. This also applies when cutting meat or vegetables for kebabs.
- Never salt meat before cooking because it will release its juices, thus ruining the caramelisation process so essential to good flavour and cause the meat to toughen and dry out.
- Always cut incisions into the fat of chops and steaks. This prevents the grease swamping the meat and hindering the cooking process. It also stops the meat from curling up.
- Beef should ideally be served blue or rare; lamb, kidneys and liver should be medium and pink; pork and veal should be well cooked.
- A well-sealed grill does not mean charred and burnt! So take care that your fire is stabilised before you begin to cook. Flames and smoke must not lick around the meat.
- Whereas you should never salt meat before you cook it, the reverse is true with fish. Always salt it before you put it on the grill and always turn it frequently, at least four times if it is big and at least twice if it is small.
- If you are cleaning your own fish, whenever possible cut through its natural orifices rather than slitting the whole body open. It is a little difficult, but worth it. And always replace the gut with some fresh herbs.